BRITAIN IN OLD PHOTOGRAPHS

HALIFAX PUBS

Old Cock Hotel.

BRITAIN IN OLD PHOTOGRAPHS

HALIFAX PUBS

STEPHEN GEE

The Old King Cross Inn.

First published 2008
The History Press Ltd.
The Mill, Brimscombe Port
Stroud, Gloucestershire, GL5 2QG
www.thehistorypress.co.uk

Reprinted 2012

© Stephen Gee, 2008

The right of Stephen Gee to be identified as the Author of this work has been asserted in accordance with the Copyrights, Designs and Patents Act 1988.

All rights reserved. No part of this book may be reprinted or reproduced or utilised in any form or by any electronic, mechanical or other means, now known or hereafter invented, including photocopying and recording, or in any information storage or retrieval system, without the permission in writing from the Publishers.
British Library Cataloguing in Publication Data.
A catalogue record for this book is available from the British Library.

ISBN 978 0 7524 4811 4

Typesetting and origination by The History Press.
Printed in Great Britain

CONTENTS

	Acknowledgements	6
	Introduction	7
1.	Halifax Town Centre	9
2.	Around Halifax	25
3.	North of Halifax	37
4.	Brighouse and Surrounding Areas	53
5.	Elland and Surrounding Districts	65
6.	Down the Calder Valley	77
7.	Sowerby Bridge and the Ryburn Valley	89
8.	The Breweries	105
9.	Halifax Artists	117

ACKNOWLEDGEMENTS

This book would not have been possible without the photographers, artists and local historians who over the years have recorded the history of the Halifax Parish and, in particular for this book, that of the pubs and breweries, to these I would like to record my thanks. I would also like to extend my thanks to the staff at Calderdale Central Library for their assistance during my research and to those at our local papers who continue to produce a valuable record of local events.

I would also like to thank the many people who have helped me with the book, many unaware of the reason, as I took the opportunity to question them on pubs, breweries and local happenings.

Finally I would like to extend a special acknowledgement and thanks to my partner Joyce who has not only had the patience to put up with me during my research but also for reading, encouraging and supporting me during the writing of the book.

Ready for the off, these ladies are on a charabanc parked outside the Orange Tree, Cross Street. Webster's acquired the Orange Tree in 1933 as part of the takeover of Joseph Stocks, Shibden Head Brewery.

INTRODUCTION

The brewing industry, and the public houses and inns that go with it, has a history stretching back several hundred years within the Parish of Halifax. We are fortunate that past historians have recorded events and incidents that allow us to gain a picture of pub life going back many years. We have also had several local artists such as John Horner and Joseph Rideal Smith who produced portfolios containing views of Halifax including its inns. Complementing these is the large number of photographs that have survived over the years of our local pubs and breweries.

Some of the earliest references to local brewing go back as far as 1307, when the wife of Thomas of the Hall was presented to the Sheriff's Turn in Halifax for illegal brewing and fined 12d. Another five women were fined that day for the same misdemeanour. At that time the selling price of ale was regulated by the market price of corn and on the fourth conviction culprits would be 'set on the pillory without redemption'. In 1406, William Otes, Thomas Gibson, Richard Lister, Henry of the Wood and Isabel Lister were presented at the Turn, for brewing 'help-ales' and selling at an illegal profit. In those days help ales were brewed gratuitously, for church and charitable purposes, and sold for the benefit of the poor.

In 1539, we find a further reference to drinking habits, in a document presented to the steward of the Manor of Wakefield:

> Alle ye Hole Inhabytantes off Halyfaxe, in regard to misconduct of certain persons on festive occasions, also here ys sertan mysorderyd pepyll, yt [that] none honest men can be, or resort to make mery, and drynke ther monay butt to have qwarelles pykyd apon them, and ether to take a shame, or elles to breke ys kunges peace – desyrynge yowe yt ye offyeeresse a reformacyon for ye same.

Moving forward to the eighteenth century, John Caygill carried out a survey in 1735, recording that Halifax had one malt kiln, one brew house, twenty inns or public houses, one alehouse and one pipehouse. The Cross Inn (Union Cross) then had a bowling green; the Cock Inn (Old Cock) had two closes of land; the Swan Inn (White Swan) had a warehouse and garden at the rear. Other pubs listed included the Common House Inn, Woolshops; Broadstone Inn, Southgate; Seven Stars Inn, Back Lane and the Horns Inn, next to the Goal House in Goal Lane.

The eighteenth century proved to be a colourful period for our local pubs, with many of them involved in the criminal underworld. Foremost was the activity of the coiners, who would clip the edges of coins and use the clippings to produce counterfeit coins. Who better to provide good coins for clipping but the landlords at the time? The Cragg Vale coiners' leader, David Hartley, was arrested at the Old Cock and subsequently hanged at Tyburn, near York, on 28 April 1770. Two of his 'gang', Robert Thomas and Matthew

Normanton, planned the murder of excise man William Deighton whilst in the Dusty Miller, Mytholmroyd. They too were hanged in York, their bodies later suspended in chains on Beacon Hill. During the ensuing investigations many pubs and inns were left, rather swiftly, without their landlords, as many took the opportunity to abscond rather than face trial and potentially the noose or transportation.

Another accomplice instrumental in the killing of Deighton was Thomas Spencer; however, Spencer survived until 1783, when, on 7 June that year, he led a mob into Halifax as part of the corn riots and demanded Mr Anderton, the landlord of the Boar's Head, to hand over the corn from his warehouse. On his refusal Spencer went through the town commandeering corn wagons and selling the contents to the mob, at a price set by himself. Spencer was later convicted and hanged on Beacon Hill, where the remains of Thomas and Normanton were still hanging in their chains.

Moving into the nineteenth century there is a curious entry in the *Mercury* of 29 November 1806, where we find a Halifax publican was convicted and fined £5 for using tobacco instead of hops to brew ale.

The Piece Hall Sings that commenced in 1831 have been well documented, although the dispensing of beer to the Sunday School children to 'slake their thirst' during the early jubilees seems to get overlooked. Clearly a different attitude existed in those days towards drink.

In the first half of the nineteenth century, elections often caused feelings to run high, and the 1832 parliamentary elections in Halifax were no exception. During the elections, it is recorded that the town was at the mercy of a mob not less than 500 who rampaged through the town, apparently accompanied by music, and caused extensive damage to properties, including many pubs. By the time a troop of lancers arrived from Dewsbury, the mob had done their damage and had already dispersed. The resulting claims for damages give us a list of the many public houses affected: Three Pigeons – £30, King of Prussia – £15, Shakespeare – £5 11s, White Horse – £6 9s 10d, Black Bull – £3, plus many more, making total damages of over £240.

Three years later in 1835, John Horner produced his portfolio of Halifax views and these, along with those of his fellow artists and the photographers who captured our local pubs, pub trips, the landlords and regulars, all help to bring to life the history of the pubs and breweries in Halifax.

1

HALIFAX TOWN CENTRE

A smart set of gents outside the Union Cross Hotel. The postcard was posted to Mr Tom Shepley of the Clarence Hotel, Blackpool, with the simple message, 'do you recognise any of the boys?' The postcard was dated 22 August 1910. On exactly the same day in 1748, John Wesley had attempted to preach from the Market Cross but had to abandon his attempts when he met with 'violence and interruption' from the vast crowd, forcing him to move to a more receptive area in Skircoat Green.

The Union Cross Hotel is the oldest inn in Halifax, dating back almost 500 years, when it was called simply 'The Cross' due to its position opposite the Market Cross in Old Market. Records refer to Richard Lister of the Cross in 1535. The 'Union' part of the name was added around 1745 at the time of the Jacobite Rebellion which had roused patriotic feelings throughout the country in defence of the 'Altar and the Throne'.

The occasion is unknown but it is a very smart turnout by the staff of the White Swan Hotel on Princess Street. The present hotel was opened in 1858 but the Swan, as it was originally known, has a history going back several hundred years when the inn was located on Crown Street. Records refer to Anthony Foxcroft living at the Swan in 1585. In 1643, during the Civil War, reference is made to James Foxcroft, of the Swan, as the constable. In the *Memoirs of Captain John Hodgson of Coley Hall*, he refers to being arrested in August 1665, on Market Day in Halifax, and being carried to the Swan.

The Hop Pole Inn closed in 1915 and was demolished shortly after as part of the Bull Green development. The name is fairly uncommon but a few pubs with this name still exist around the country. The name is derived from the tall pole used to support the wires on which hop plants are trained.

The earliest reference to the Lower George was in an account book at Shibden Hall, 1704, where it was recorded, 'Mr George Wilkinson of the Lower George' paid 2s 4d for 1lb of anchovies. The pub was demolished in 1972.

The oval sign attached to the gable end of the property on the left is for the White Horse Inn, Southgate. The photograph was taken in around 1894 when Joshua Sutcliffe was the landlord. On the corner of Albion Street is a fine display of posters advertising, amongst other places, trips to Blackpool. The White Horse was demolished in 1898 as part of improvements and widening of Southgate. The pub was rebuilt in its current position and was opened on 24 June 1899.

Another view of Southgate, this time looking towards the Town Hall, a scene that shows how narrow Southgate once was. The White Horse is on the right and across the other side of Albion Street was the Greyhound Inn. The Greyhound was demolished in 1892 to make way for the New Borough Market.

Three of Halifax's old pubs are pictured in this view showing the bottom of Russell Street prior to demolition in the early 1890s to make way for the new Borough Market, which opened in 1896. On the right of the picture is the Duke of York, in Russell Street, whilst the Saddle Inn was round the corner on Market Street. During the Napoleonic War the Saddle Inn was renowned as a recruiting centre, where shillings were dropped into tankards of ale to entice locals to enlist. Many went off to fight in the Battle of Trafalgar and later with Wellington at Waterloo. On the extreme left, the Wheat Sheaf can just be seen, now the Portman and Pickles.

This is a delivery being made to the new Saddle Inn from Brear & Brown, whose brewery was at Hipperholme. The Saddle was incorporated in the building of the new Borough Market, its position being slightly moved to the corner of Market Street and Russell Street where Farnell's butcher's shop was previously located. The Saddle closed in 1966.

BREWERS
CELLAR

PLUMMET LINE HOTEL
TAXIS
Take a TG taxi!
T.G
TAXIS
PREMIER MILK BAR
Milk Bar

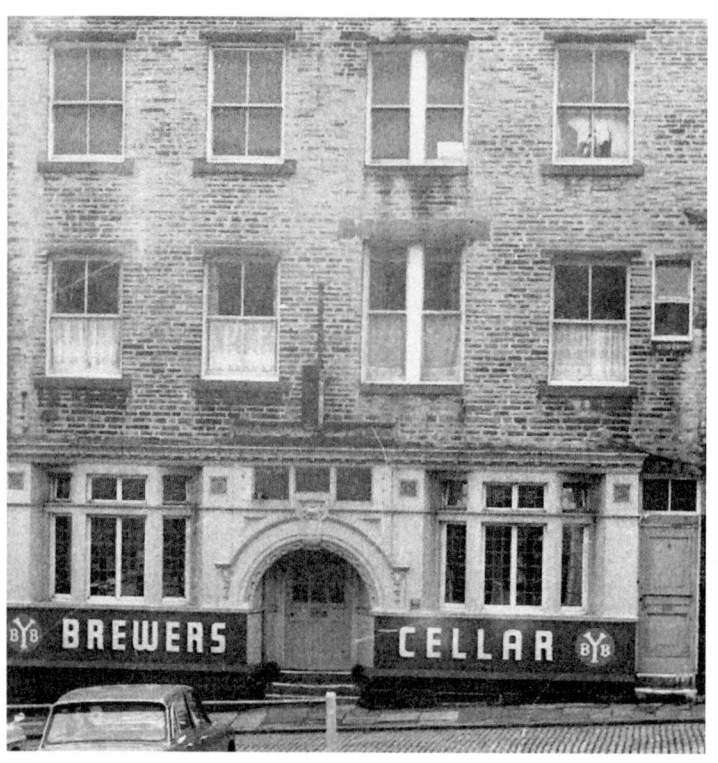

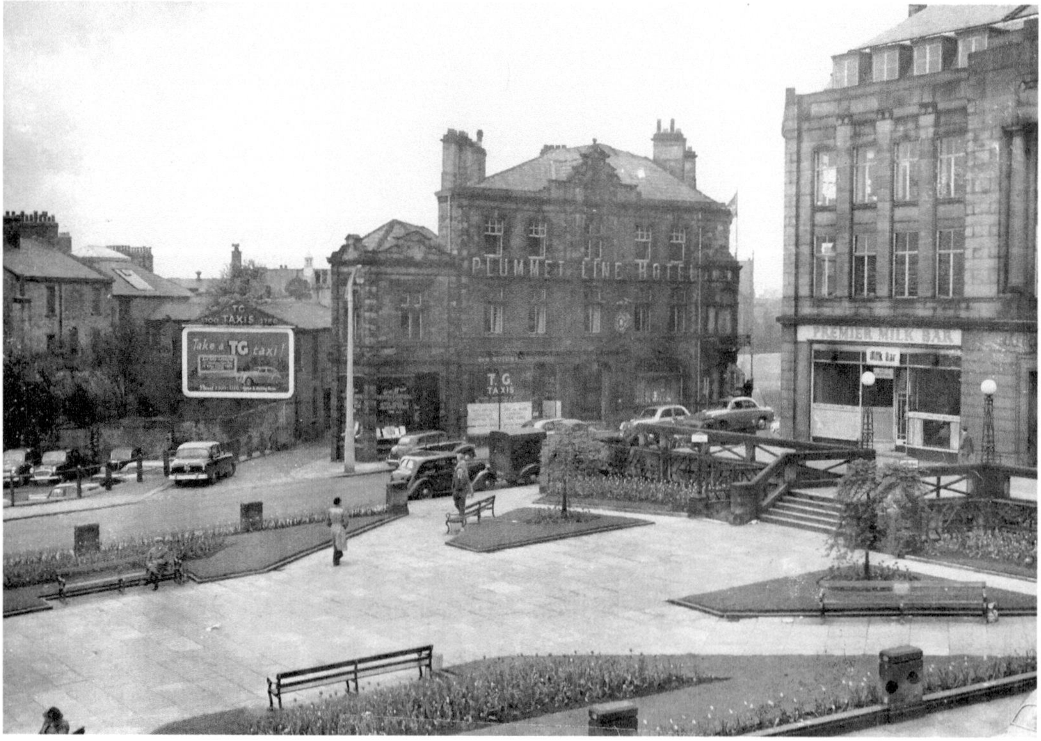

This photograph of the Duke William Inn at Clark Bridge, Bank Bottom was taken in 1963, two years before the pub closed. Under the railway arch is Lower Kirkgate and the parish church. In Revd Thomas Wright's 1738 book, *The Antiquities of the Town of Halifax*, he refers to the Halifax Gibbet Law: 'if a felon after condemnation and sentence pass'd upon them they managed to escape out of the Forest of Hardwick, (which Liberty on the East End of the Town doth not extend above the breadth of a small rivulet), the Bailiff of Halifax has no power to apprehend them'. A newspaper article fifty years ago stated that if an offender had reached the Duke William Inn, he had achieved sanctuary – however I am sure, on the fear of losing one's head, you would not have stopped to find out if you had passed the border. Even more, you would not have returned like the unfortunate John Lacy who, as Wright describes, 'after his escape liv'd seven years out of the forest, yet coming afterwards boldly within the Liberties was retaken, and executed upon his former Verdict and Condemnation. His Name is enter'd in the Register in the following words: John Lacy *perditissimus Nebulo et Latro decollatus, Januarij* 26, 1623.'

Opposite above: The Brewers Cellar was located in Wade Street. In its back yard there used to be two relics of olden days. One was a carved stone showing a malt shovel, which was once the sign for the ancient Malt Shovel Inn that was located on Northgate as far back as 1629. The second was an old converted gas lamp. Whether either of these curiosities survived following its closure in 1975 and subsequent demolition, is not known.

Opposite below: Following much debate at the council meeting held on 1 December 1897, it was agreed to pay £3,000 for the rebuilding of the Plummet Line as part of the Bull Close Lane improvement scheme. The new Plummet Line was built the following year, 1898. Apparently a stipulation exists stating that there must always be a Plummet Line on the site, and therefore the new building had to be built whilst the old Plummet Line was still operating – this meant that for a short period two Plummet Lines occupied the site.

A rare photograph of the Bee Hive Inn that was located at No. 33 King Cross Street. The procession is possibly part of the celebrations for Queen Victoria's Diamond Jubilee in June 1897. The Bee Hive closed in 1932.

Swift's Home Brewed Ales is clearly advertised on the old Cross Keys Inn in King Cross Street. The rear of the inn led into Spice Cake Lane where Henry Swift ran his brewery. His son, George, built and ran the Falcon Brewery at Salterhebble. The family also ran the nearby Beehive Inn. Both these pubs were demolished due to development and road widening activity in the area and a new building was erected under the combined name of the Beehive and Cross Keys Inn, opening in 1933.

The inn displaying the Webster's sign is the old Bull's Head Hotel, Bull Green. It was here in 1738 that the Masonic Lodge of Probity was founded. These buildings were demolished in the late 1930s as part of the George Street improvement scheme. Although considerable delays occurred due to the Second World War, Arthur Hoyle, the landlord, moved to his new premises in 1940.

A lot of activity in this photograph of Bull Green showing the Crown and Anchor on the left and the new Bull's Head in the centre. The architects for the building were local firm Jackson & Fox. During previous years, the company had been involved in many designs for Webster's including the White Horse (1899) and the New Talbot (1926). The new Bull's Head opened on 28 August 1940.

The Ramsden's sign to the right is at the entrance to the Upper George Yard from Cheapside. Perhaps the most infamous tenant of the inn was Joseph Hanson, who was also the deputy constable of Halifax when he was arrested in 1769, for diminishing the gold coin of the kingdom. When arrested by Francis Simpson, of Bradford, he managed to persuade Simpson to allow him to go back to his inn to complete some important affairs. Whilst there, the bailiff was distracted by an accomplice and Hanson made his escape; despite twenty guineas reward, advertised in the *Leeds Mercury*, he was never seen again.

Looking down the Old Cock Yard towards the Old Cock Hotel, one of the most historic inns of Halifax. Many organisations have met or were founded at the inn including the Harmonic Club, Loyal Georgian Society, the Freemasons, the Music Club and the Halifax Building Society. Many famous people are known to have frequented the Old Cock (including Branwell Brontë, whom the landlord had to send a summons to Haworth to get him to pay his outstanding bill). It was here on Saturday 14 October 1769 that David Hartley, 'King David', the leader of the Cragg Vale Coiners was arrested.

The Boar's Head Hotel on Southgate was one of four public houses built into the new Halifax Borough Market that was opened in 1896. The other three were the Peacock, closed in 1961, the Wheat Sheaf, now Portman and Pickles, and the Saddle, which was demolished to make way for the Yorkshire Electricity Board showrooms in 1966.

Prior to the present Halifax Town Hall opening in 1863, the Town Council held its meetings at various locations. The entry in the council minutes of 6 August 1849 reads, 'holden at the Town Hall in Union Street' – this was in the building opposite the Town Hall Tavern, the pub that can be seen on the right of this photograph. The Tavern is now known as the Westgate.

Historian Revd John Watson in his *History of Halifax*, 1775, refers to Daniel Defoe, who was said to have written his famous book *Robinson Crusoe* whilst staying at the Rose and Crown in Halifax – but which Rose and Crown? In the nineteenth century, E.J. Walker, known then as an authority on the subject, stated that the Sportsman, seen here on Upper Crown Street, was known as the Rose and Crown at the end of the eighteenth century, then the Coopers Arms before taking its present name. The Grand Junction Hotel, built in 1864, can also be seen located at the bottom of Pellon Lane.

The New Talbot opened on 22 October 1926. This was another inn designed by local firm Jackson & Fox and was rebuilt during a period where the Halifax breweries were very active in rebuilding and carrying out modifications to their properties. The New Talbot, a Webster's house, closed in 1974 and was demolished in 1979 as part of the Woolshops' redevelopment.

Set in the shadow of the parish church, from which it derives its name, is the Ring O'Bells Inn. The inn was built around 1720 and originally known as the Sign of the Church Inn. In the cellars are traces of masonry going back to the thirteenth century, and in one of the walls there is a gravestone from 1635. The cars are parked in the space left following demolition of two seventeenth-century cottages in 1949 that had become structurally unsafe. The building at the top was the Waterhouse Almshouses.

John Hanson was the landlord of the Britannia Inn, Woolshops when this photograph was taken near the turn of the last century. The Britannia Inn closed in 1954.

The stocks and the Old West Gateway to Halifax Parish church can be seen in this photograph taken during the demolition of the Church Tavern. The pub closed in 1892; the last landlord was G. Robinson. John Murgatroyd was landlord in 1874 and had nine daughters.

This party are posing outside the Crown Hotel near the bottom of Horton Street. The fairly ornate window in the background is still present on today's Imperial Crown Hotel but the sign now states, 'The Wallis and Simpson Restaurant'.

Situated in the shadow of a rival brewery, the Corporation Inn was located on Corporation Street close to Whitaker's Brewery. The Ramsden's house closed in 1969 and along with all the property in the area was later demolished to make way for the town's inner relief road.

Harry Calvert was the landlord of the Stannary Inn when this photograph was taken. The inn was situated on the corner of Green Lane and Stannary Lane. This is where Richard Whitaker first lived when he came to Halifax in 1848. He started his brewing business here, albeit on a small scale, until his brewery was opened in Corporation Street. The Stannary Inn closed in 1967.

Left: Located opposite the Corporation Inn at the corner of Corporation Street and Crib Lane was the Smith's Arms. The pub first opened in 1874, selling the beer from the nearby Whitaker's Brewery. In 1967 it closed its doors for the last time, another victim of the demolition to make way for the inner relief road.

Below: The Lamb Inn was located at the Halifax railway station. The notice on the counter states 'The Hotels Executive British Transport beg to advise passengers that on and from the 1 March 1950, this establishment will be closed.' A recent correspondent to the *Halifax Courier* referred to the Lamb Inn as, 'the first pub in Halifax that you had to pay to get in, by buying either a train or platform ticket'.

2

AROUND HALIFAX

A superb photograph of the Old King Cross Inn taken when George W. Wright was the landlord. A fairly cramped horse-drawn charabanc is packed for a lad's day out. I'm not sure where they were going, but for the horse's sake let's hope there were not too many hills to climb. The Old King closed in 1975.

Another picture from an Old King Cross Inn collection that shows the pub was also popular for celebrations. This one was for the Coronation of King Edward VII in 1902.

The Junction Hotel on the corner of King Cross Road and Queen's Road, decorated for the Coronation of King Edward VII in 1902. Sarah Roberts was the landlady at the time and it is probable that this is Sarah posing for the camera outside the pub.

Right: The Queen's Road Tavern, No. 217 Queen's Road was bought by Webster's from Mary Priestley and John Collier in 1884. This picture is taken when James Priestley was the landlord.

Below: Looking up Haugh Shaw Road from its junction with Paradise Row, the Royal Oak, a Ramsden's pub, can be seen on the right. All this property was demolished in the 1970s to make way for the King Cross bypass (or, as it was later named, the Aachen Way).

The Brown Cow, Gibbet Street was created in the middle of the nineteenth century by converting a row of cottages as seen in this rather damp view of the inn. Mary Howarth was the landlady when the photograph was taken. Prior to this, William Howarth is listed as running the beerhouse in trade directories of 1894 and 1905.

An outing from the Bowling Green Hotel, in 1906. The landlord at the time was Jack Riley who played rugby for Halifax and was part of the highly successful team that achieved the double in 1902/3, winning the League Championship and the Challenge Cup; the team retained the cup the following year, beating Warrington 8-3 in the final. Adverts for the Bowling Green at the time stated that the pub was three minutes (direct tram route) from the football ground – it is likely these gents were going a bit further.

The Horse and Jockey Inn at the junction of Gibbet Street and Warley Road, Highroad Well. This picture was taken in around 1905 when James Farrar was the landlord.

Seen here not long after being rebuilt, the Golden Lion Hotel at Highroad Well. The pub was rebuilt slightly further back from the location of its predecessor, of the same name, which was demolished in 1901. The banner on the windows indicate the pub had a Commercial Room, a Bar Parlour and, to the right, a Smoke Room.

Quite a large crowd assembled outside the Prince of Wales Feathers Inn at King Cross. The man in the foreground appears slightly elevated from the rest and looks to be conducting, perhaps for the King Cross Prize Band. The pub, formerly a Joseph Stocks house, was rebuilt in the late 1920s, realigning the property with others, and the name shortened to the Feathers. Local architects Scott & Bagnall designed the new building.

Numerous streets and roads once surrounded the Trafalgar Inn, King Cross. However, in the 1970s a massive clearing exercise saw many of these disappear and as a result the frontage of the pub was opened to the new Aachen Way. The surrounding area known as Trafalgar predates the pub, the name appearing on early maps. The first known reference to the pub is in a 1905 directory, 100 years after the famous battle.

Another inn designed by architects Jackson & Fox, the Allan Fold, was built in 1939 on the site of an old house that dated back to 1654. The façade of the original house has been preserved in the wall facing Burnley Road. The pub opened on 5 April 1939 following the transfer of the license from the Brown Cow, Burnley Road.

About to set out for the Dukeries, a charabanc with ladies from the Thorn Tree Inn, Gibbet Street. The message on this postcard stated that they were on a day outing to the ancestral home of Lady Elizabeth's mother, the Duke of Portland's place, located 140 miles away. The party left Halifax at 6.30 a.m. and arrived back at 9.45 p.m. Harry Normington was the landlord of the pub when this picture was taken.

No prizes for guessing the date of this photograph showing the Queen's Road Hotel. The tramcar is decorated to celebrate the Silver Jubilee of King George V in 1935. The pub, which was later known as the Queen's Road End, closed in 2000.

Halifax Corporation's first motor bus, outside the New Inn, Mount Tabor on 14 October 1912. The New Inn was one of the few houses that were once owned by the nearby Springhead Brewery. The inn is reputed to have had an underground passage linked directly to the brewery. The brewery was founded by John Aspinall in 1853, and closed in 1932.

This procession from Christ Church Sunday School, Mount Pellon, has just passed the Wheat Sheaf pub at the end of Brackenbed Lane. The sign on the side of the pub is for the Halifax Cricket & Football Club Annual Sports, stating 'First Class Entries' and 'All The Champions'; the sign is dated June 1904.

The Royal was originally known as West Air and was built as the home of John Edward Wainhouse, in 1877. The building was designed by Richard Dugdale, who a few years earlier had designed the upper sections of Wainhouse's more famous tower. Wainhouse lived at West Air until his death in 1883.

In support of the Chartist movement, the landlord of the then Waggoners Inn announced, 'the people of Skircoat Green shall join in that march of freedom and I will raise the Standard of Freedom at this inn'; and he renamed the inn accordingly. The movement received huge support from the area, an indication being the meeting held on Good Friday 1848 when approximately 20,000 Chartists gathered on Skircoat Moor, the largest gathering held in Yorkshire that year, to listen to speeches from, amongst others, Ben Rushton, Joseph Barker, and Kit Shackleton (county secretary of the movement). The proceedings were watched over by 500 special constables.

For the passing trade who have climbed the steep Salterhebble Hill, the Staffords' Arms has provided a welcome stop for many years. In the first Halifax trade directory, produced by Walker in 1845, James Fox is listed as the landlord of the inn; at the time this picture was taken, around 1910, Arthur Crossley was the licensee.

Already in a state of demolition, this is the Navigation Inn at the bottom of Salterhebble Hill in 1901. The last landlord was Fred Whitaker. There were several pubs either at the bottom, on the way up or at the top of Salterhebble – the steepness of the hill dictating several stops being necessary.

Plenty of activity in front of the Punch Bowl Inn, passing traders having a rest before either climbing Salterhebble Hill, Exley Bank or taking the gentler route towards Elland or West Vale. Over the years, apart from passing trade, the pub benefited from the rugby crowd when Salterhebble played on a pitch at the top of Exley Bank. In 1919, Halifax Town moved to play on the same pitch after finding their field at Sandhall, Highroad Well occupied by Asquiths.

This photograph shows the rear of the old Volunteer's Arms, Copley. The landlord at the time of this photograph was James Gledhill. Copley Old Hall, which stood on the site, was partially demolished in the latter part of the eighteenth century. (The remainder, seen here, became the village inn.) This itself was demolished in 1915, to make way for the present building.

Taken at the front of the Volunteer's Arms and ready for an outing on a horse-drawn wagonette. The photograph dates from around 1905, when Joe Lees was the landlord.

3

NORTH OF HALIFAX

Landlady Ada Thornton stands on the steps of the Who Could Have Thought It Inn in Southowram. Later the name was given more of a Yorkshire translation and changed to Ba Gum Who'd 'a' Thowt It Inn'. The Ramsden's house closed in 1933. The building, on Waterclough Lane, was demolished in 1941.

At least three pubs that are no longer with us can be seen in this picture of New Bank: the Wellington on the immediate left, the Pineapple, whose sign is visible further down on the same side of the road, and the Great Northern Hotel on the right all closed in 1968 to make way for road improvements.

Sour Milk Hall, once a farmhouse, was located on Horley Green Road. It was here on 21 December 1738 that Dan Taylor was born. At the age of five, Dan worked with his father Azor in a coal mine under Beacon Hill, rarely seeing the sun apart from Sundays. Despite this, even at this early age, Dan was an able reader, astounding people at his ability to read from the Bible. In 1762, he left the coal pit and moved to Wadsworth, where he set up a school room for teaching and preaching. In 1763 he was ordained to the 'Pastoral Office'; the following year he was responsible for building the Baptist church at Birchcliffe. In 1770, along with ten other ministers, he established the 'New Connexion of General Baptists'. Sour Milk Hall closed as a pub in the 1960s.

Granville, Hazel and Gordon Bowmer, with the Red Lion at Ploughcroft behind them. One of the most famous regulars of the Red Lion was Percy Shaw, inventor of the reflective road studs better known as cats' eyes. The building burnt down some years ago.

Taken in the 1930s, these gents are sat outside the Prospect Inn, Cowroyd Place, Range Bank. The landlord at the time was John H. Hillary who is in the middle of the front row. The Prospect was one of the twenty Daniel Fielding houses that transferred to Webster's when they bought the White Castle Brewery in 1961.

No need to guess who got the prize for the best collar. This young lad and gents are stood outside the Sportsman Inn at Ploughcroft. Ralph Demain was the landlord at the time; his family ran the inn from 1896 to 1938.

Still outside the Sportsman, but now under the license of Kate Demain. Ralph and Kate's son, John is in the doorway on the left, with the trilby. Edgar Mitchell, who became the landlord after Kate Demain, is on the far left of the middle row. The inn got its name from the various sports it has accommodated over the years: hunting in the Shibden Valley, knur and spell, cricket and more recently, skiing, when in the 1980s an artificial ski slope was built on the site.

Formerly a Joseph Stocks house, the Brickmakers Arms, New Bank was taken over by Webster's in 1933. The pub, whose name reflects the nearby industries with several fireclay and brickworks in the area, closed in 1969. The buildings, which formed part of a wedge shape, known locally as 'Coffin Row', were demolished in 1978.

On its way to Brighouse, the tram is approaching the Stump Cross Inn. A pub of the same name was buried when Godley cutting was made in 1830. During its construction an article in the *Halifax Commercial Chronicle*, September 1829, describes the inn as follows: 'judging from its appearance, it has held out its hospitable shelter to the weary traveller in time – lang syne'. At the time it was still tenanted, but the stones and earth from Godley cutting were only 21yds from the door. The landlord, who remained until the old inn was almost buried, had already started the building of the present inn, 'further up the road'. On the opposite side of the road is the Museum Hotel.

Shibden Mill was the ancient manorial corn mill mentioned in the Wakefield Court Rolls as far back as 1308. The history of the mill and adjoining properties including the mill house, which would later become the Shibden Mill Inn, was well documented by the Halifax historian John Lister. His ancestors had long been associated with, and eventually owned, the mill, as far back as the 1660s. In 1772, William Lister sold the property to William Walker of Crownest, Lightcliffe. In a detailed inventory of the estate there was no mention of a public house and the mill was still a corn mill. Dorothy Bottomley was then tenant and later the Bottomley family converted the premises to a worsted mill. It is likely the Bottomleys were also responsible for turning part of the premises into a public house. In 1838, Sarah Bottomley was listed as running the Board Inn in Shibden. Four years later, in 1842, Sarah Bottomley was running the Shibden Mill Inn and the Board Inn was no longer mentioned. This would suggest that the inn was originally called the Board Inn. Board Inns, still in existence around the country, derive their name from the above period, when following the Beerhouse Act of 1830, for a fee of two guineas, householders were allowed to sell beer. However, they were only allowed to display a board over their doors bearing the landlord's name, i.e. not a sign.

A view of the mill dam at the Shibden Mill Inn, in its years as a boating lake. The dam was filled in during the first half of the last century and is now used as a car park. John Lister in his 1911 paper on the mill, states, 'The mill-wheel has long been silent, the townsmen no longer meet here to lay rates and make assessments. The old order has changed, and what was once a central place of business, is now one of pleasure, beer and boats.'

The Museum Hotel in the days when it was a Stocks house and long before the nearby Shibden Hall was converted to a museum. Over the years it has often been stated that the pub derived its name from the nearby museum, which is clearly incorrect. Some years back a regular of the pub related a more likely story that the pub was once called the Delvers Arms but was renamed the Museum Hotel by a previous landlord who was keen on taxidermy and used a room, below the pub, for his displays.

The Shoulder of Mutton, Northowram comprises of a number of buildings with different architecture, as seen in this photograph. The building on the right was built by Nathaniel Priestley in 1723 and was known as Priestley Hall. In Revd Mark Pearson's *History of Northowram*, 1898, he refers to the middle section as 'no doubt, originally the farm in connection with the mansion'.

A wintry day for landlord John Bolland, who is looking out from the steps of the Queen Victoria, Bradford Road, Northowram. The pub was built in 1837 and in early directories it is listed simply as the Victoria Inn; Benjamin Fawthrop was the landlord in 1842, with William Fawthrop taking over by 1845.

Bus No. 9, on its way to Halifax, is stopped outside the Bank Top Inn, Ovenden. The inn was one of two located at Bank Top that closed in 1971.

Dating back to the 1840s when James Butterworth was the landlord, the Broad Tree was the second pub at Bank Top to close in 1971.

The Noah's Ark Inn, Ovenden was purchased by Webster's, in 1860. The inn was reputed to have been the last beerhouse in Halifax to apply for a full license.

Standing outside the Railway Hotel at the bottom of Nursery Lane, Ovenden. These gents are ready to go and support Halifax at Wembley in the Rugby League Challenge Cup Final against Warrington in 1954. The match ended in a 4-4 draw with the replay being played at Odsal, in front of a crowd officially numbered at 102,000 but unofficially stated to be well above 120,000.

John Brearcliffe built Little Moor, now the Ivy House Inn, in 1704. In 1845 James Riley occupied the premises as a farmer and tailor. By 1881 the name had changed to the Ivy House Inn with Elijah Lister listed as the landlord; the license from the nearby King of Prussia public house being transferred to the inn. Elijah Lister was also listed as a beer retailer in 1874, but no location is given.

The horse and carts are standing outside the Queen's Head Inn, Mason's Green. It was reported back in 1949 that the Ovenden District was one in which nicknames were applied not only to people but also to premises and land. The older inhabitants had known the inn for many years as 'Hen's Face'. It was from Mason Green, on 14 February 1939, that Halifax Corporation ran its last tram.

This picture shows the Commercial Inn, Illingworth clearly advertising the ales of Daniel Fielding, who operated from the White Castle Brewery, Bradshaw. The picture was taken prior to the inn being rebuilt in the 1930s.

The architect for the new Commercial Inn at Illingworth was H. Wilkinson of Walsh & Maddock. The inn reopened in 1937, still under Fielding's ownership. The licensee at the time of this photograph was Leonard Ambler, who advertised 'Our Usual Service – The Best'. The ownership of the inn was transferred to Webster's when they acquired the White Castle Brewery in 1961.

There have been many famous visitors to Halifax, but perhaps one of the most famous (yet secretive) visits was made by the Beatles in 1964, following their show in Bradford. The Beatles stayed at Holdsworth House, then known as the Cavalier Country Club, on 9 October 1964. This photograph is one of only a few pictures that exist of the stay: the rest of the series, and full story, can be seen in Trevor Simpson's excellent book, *Small Town Saturday Night*.

Abraham Brigg built Holdsworth House in 1633 to replace a timbered house that had stood on the site since the middle of the fifteenth century. Although the original hall still remains relatively intact, there have been many alterations and additions throughout the last 400 years. Abraham Brigg himself lived in the hall for twenty years before selling it to Henry Wadsworth in 1657. He then moved to Halifax, where, according to the diaries of Oliver Heywood, he kept an alehouse, drank much, fed excessively and died in February 1671.

The Talbot Inn at Illingworth dates back to the fifteenth century, when, tradition states, it was used by soldiers during the Wars of the Roses. The house was used as a hostelry before becoming the vicarage to St Mary's and reverted back to a pub around the time when the main Keighley Road was completed in 1785. The pub, then a Ramsden's house, was demolished in the 1930s, and a new Talbot Inn was built on the site.

The Brewers Arms, Moor End Road, Mount Tabor, photographed in around 1905 when Thomas Morley was the landlord. The pub closed only a few years later, in 1911.

This photograph cried out to be included in a book related to drink. These gents seem to have had a nice little business going in Cromwell Woods, Southowram – obviously helping themselves to some XXX bitter. Another barrel and cart can just be seen on the left, so was this one of the early microbreweries?

Waiting to set off en route to the Town Hall, tramcar No. 42 stands outside the Blue Bell Inn, Bank Top, Southowram. Webster's purchased the Blue Bell in 1877; the pub closed just under thirty years later, on 14 February 1906.

The gent in the bottom left corner enjoys a quick puff on his pipe whilst landlord Joseph Rushworth and his wife stand in the doorway of the Shoulder of Mutton, Southowram. The photograph dates from around 1900.

The Manor House Inn, Bank Top, Southowram in the days when Friend Priestley, the landlord, was licensed to sell 'all intoxicating liquor'. Over the years many different organisations used the inn for meetings; the small sign on the left indicates that the Royal Antediluvian Order of Buffaloes, the R.A.O.B., met at the inn every Friday. In the 1930s, the Old Rishworthians used the pub for changing, when they played at Southowram, and some years later the Southowram Home Guard also met at the inn. The Manor House closed in 2002 and was demolished the following year.

4

BRIGHOUSE AND SURROUNDING AREAS

The George Hotel was built in 1815 by a Dr Day. Perhaps an ancestor, Peter Day ran the Malt Kiln in Brighouse, in 1769. In this photograph, Dyson's 'Home Brewed Sparkling Ales and Stout' is advertised on the brewery that was attached to the pub. James Dyson took over the business from Henry Lockwood in 1889.

The poster on the Wellington Inn, Briggate advertises the Yorkshire Challenge Cup match between Manningham and Brighouse Rangers on 27 March 1894. The Wellington closed in 1947 and was demolished the following year. And the match – it was the first time that season that Rangers lost at their Lane Head ground; however, revenge was sweet when, in the following season, Rangers beat Manningham in the semi-final and went on to beat Morley in the final, 16-4 in front of 20,000 spectators at Headingley.

The Black Bull Hotel was built in 1740. In the first Brighouse Brewster session in 1899, the superintendent of police stated that Brighouse was one of the most drunken towns in the Halifax police district. By 1904, the 'Bench' were given power to refer cases for extinction of license on the grounds of non-necessity; the police and authorities were to use this actively over the next few decades to close many pubs in the town. The Black Bull itself was referred in 1936 but was reprieved.

The original Prince of Wales was pulled down in 1924 as part of a road-widening scheme. Designed by Jackson & Fox, the new building was opened on 1 April 1927. The building incorporated timber from the wooden battleship HMS *Donegal*. Renowned carver H.P. Jackson of Coley was engaged to carve the bracketed owls at the front of the pub, representing Wisdom of the Wise, the Fool, Wine and Woman.

Crowds line the street outside the Armytage Arms, Clifton to welcome HRH Princess Louise, Duchess of Argyll, on the 22 May 1907, who was visiting Brighouse to open the Smith Art Gallery. The pub derives its name from the Armytage family, of Kirklees Hall, where the Princess had stayed as a guest for two nights.

McCarty's Prize Band pose outside the Black Bull Inn, at Clifton. These types of bands were also referred to as Waffen Fuffen bands, with many homemade instruments, fitted with reed sounding wooden mouthpieces. The founder of this band was Joe Hepworth, a cornet player, who can be seen at the front.

Another view of the Black Bull at Clifton. The gents entering the photograph from the left were leading the Coronation procession, heading off down Clifton Common, in 1911. The Black Bull closed in 1933.

It is quite rare to find old pictures depicting the inside of our local inns. This one was titled 'The Old Bar Parlour, Whitehall Hotel, Hipperholme', and shows the interior as it looked around 1800. Note the ring dangling down from the ceiling, which would suggest that these gents had been having a game of 'ringing the bull', an ancient pub game not seen very often these days.

Another photograph of the Whitehall Inn, taken when Arthur Gledhill was the landlord. The hotel gave its name to the Whitehall and Leeds Road that was completed in 1833. In 1869, the trustees of the Revd William Wilkinson, vicar of Lightcliffe, sold the inn to the Shibden Head Brewery for £1,225. The inn later became a Webster's house, when the company bought Stocks Brewery, in 1933.

I wonder how busy the Whitehall Inn was on 22 June 1911; the occasion was the Coronation of King George V and crowds throng the junction now normally full of traffic.

The Hare and Hounds, Hipperholme was purchased for £690 in 1867 by Michael Stocks, as part of the sale of the Sunderland Walker's estates. James Parker referred to the Hare and Hounds in his 1904 book, *Illustrated History from Hipperholme to Tong*, as 'an ancient hostel, which has been transformed into a modest house'. Clearly, as seen in this picture, it later reverted back to the Hare and Hounds.

The Travellers Inn, Hipperholme can be seen standing alongside Halifax Old Road. Like a lot of the property in the area, the Travellers was part of the Crow Nest estates which were sold in a three-day sale, at the New Assembly Rooms, Halifax in April 1867. The estates to be sold consisted of two mansions, houses, other properties and land close to 700 acres. Michael Stocks bought the Travellers for £1,340. The chimney, to the left of the photograph, was part of the Brear & Brown brewery.

The tram waits outside the Dusty Miller, Hove Edge on its way to Brighouse, a route that opened in June 1903. The Dusty Miller had been serving passing trade for many years previously. The Aspinall family owned the pub for quite some time. J. Aspinall is listed as the landlord in 1822 and 1838, followed by Hannah Aspinall, who is listed in 1842 and 1853.

The Sun Inn, Wakefield Road, Lightcliffe was built in 1730 for the Walker family of Crow Nest and Cliffe Hill. The inn, occupying a prime position alongside the main Halifax to Wakefield Road, would have benefited when the road was designated a turnpike in 1741. James Parker refers to the inn as 'the oldest house in the neighbourhood and would be the "Baiting House" when the stage-coaches and wagons plied from Halifax to Wakefield, before the advent of railways'. The term 'baiting' refers to a halt for refreshments, for travellers and their horses. Parker also noted that the inn was, at the time, the headquarters of the Lightcliffe Gun Club, with the Gun Club Field off Smith House Lane. The large field proved popular for other activities such as knur and spell: competitions were regularly held there and in 1919 Herbert Sykes, who had been a test pilot during the First World War, organised a Flying Week held at the Gun Club Field. This property was also sold in the 1867 sale of Sutherland Walker's estates; the inn was bought by Richard Whitaker & Sons for £870.

The Bridge End area of Brighouse was well served with local pubs. Here we can just see two of them. The first, with its ornate lantern, advertising Halifax Brewery Co. Ales and Stout, was the White Lion, which closed in 1908. Just beyond the White Lion the steps of the Star Inn can be seen, the only pub in the area still standing. The Rising Sun was located in the middle of Bramston Street, on the right; this pub also closed in 1908 and was demolished five years later in 1913.

Completing a quartet of pubs located at Bridge End, within a stone's throw of each other, was the Duke of York Inn. The Duke first opened in 1863 and was closed in 1927; its last landlord was James Bond.

The Lower George, Jumples Dyke, Rastrick was another pub that suffered as part of the ongoing redundancy campaign of the 1920s. In 1925, the inn was referred to the Brewster Session along with the Empress of India and the Freemasons' Arms. The Freemasons' Arms was reprieved but the George and Empress of India were both subsequently closed.

Brookfoot was a fairly self-contained community, with its own school, St Peter's church and also its fair share of inns and beerhouses. In the middle of this picture is the Woodman Inn on Elland Road. The inn was referred to the Brewster Sessions in 1938, declared 'redundant', and was subsequently closed.

The Wharf Inn, in the foreground of this photograph of Brookfoot, was built in the early 1830s to cater for the increasing canal traffic and to serve the growing number of mills and businesses in the area. The Calder and Hebble Canal was completed in 1770, though a cut to Halifax was not made until 1828. The pub took its present name, the Red Rooster, when the TFC Group acquired it from Webster's in 1983.

The Coley Mill Inn (on the right) was better known as t'Wheel Hoile. Both names were derived from the Old Coley Corn Mill and its large waterwheel seen on the left of this photograph. The mill, which appears in documents dating back as far as 1562, has long been demolished, but remnants of the inn can still be seen in the field below Underhill Farm.

Many photographs exist with various forms of transport passing the Punch Bowl Hotel at Bailiffe Bridge (trams, horse and carts etc), but not many feature a train, seen here crossing over Wakefield Road. In 1837, it was reported that all the ale at the Punch Bowl had been spoiled, caused by a flood, due to insufficiency of the culverts on the road above. Damages for ninety-six gallons of ale and thirty-six gallons still in the brewing pan amounted to some £15 13s.

Another view of the Punch Bowl Hotel, Bailiffe Bridge. These men are sitting on a horse-drawn charabanc belonging to John Marsh & Co., Halifax.

5

ELLAND AND SURROUNDING DISTRICTS

The Horse and Jockey, located in the shadows of the Ainley's, closed in December 1933. An interesting story was published in the *Halifax Weekly Guardian*, 5 May 1866 – 'That the public official, the bellman, much amused the people of Elland on Monday by a somewhat novel cry. He announced a sale of furniture at the Horse and Jockey, the present proprietor being about to remove. Having finished that, he again rang his bell and cried a "fine young widow", for sale, having worn three husbands'. The announcement proved a big attraction, but the 'young widow' declined to be bought.

Built as a private residence in 1689, the Rose and Crown Inn, Northgate started its connection with the brewing trade in 1858 as a coaching inn. It remained such until its closure in 1914. Following some rather poor alterations to the buildings frontage, it was converted into a warehouse and for many years was used by J. Townend & Sons, wine and spirit merchants. In 1976, a request to demolish much of the property was made, stating the building was beyond repair. Fortunately this was refused, which allowed the building to be refurbished and open once again as a pub under a succession of names including the Outside Inn, Benny's and De Lacy's.

Originally built as a farmhouse, the Wellington Inn on the right of this photograph of Southgate is one of the oldest pubs in Elland. In 1962, workmen pulling down adjoining buildings revealed some of the inn's ancient timber framework.

The Star Inn is on the right of this picture looking up New Street towards its junction with Victoria Road. The street, now demolished, was built between 1791 and 1803. It is believed the photograph shows the street decorated to celebrate the end of the First World War in 1918. The Star closed in 1966.

A photograph of Southgate, Elland showing three public houses. The first is the Blue Barrel, behind the postal worker on the left, which closed in 1965. Opposite is the Royal George, which closed in 1912, and further along Southgate, in the background, another group of people stand outside the Wellington Inn.

Another view of the Blue Barrel, this time looking back from the other side of Portland Street and much later than the previous photograph. The sign shows the pub was then a Hammonds United Brewery house, which dates the photograph to the late 1950s.

Looking down Briggate towards Elland Bridge, the New Inn can be seen on the right. The photograph is from a postcard posted in 1905. The landlord at that time was Jonathan Hall. The inn opened in 1834 and closed in 1957.

The area of Briggate was well served with public houses and two of these can be seen in this photograph, taken in the 1890s. The Malt Shovel is on the left, next to Hemingway's Saddler's shop. The Royal Hotel, on the right, dates from the 1860s and was designed by architect William Henry Crossland. The ornate sign advertises 'Billiards' and 'An Ordinary & 12.30'; 'an ordinary' was an old term for a public meal regularly provided at a set price in an eating-house or tavern. The building between the Malt Shovel and the Royal was also once a pub, the Crown and Anchor.

Mexborough's Arms is on the right of this photograph looking down Westgate. Caroline Brier was the landlady when this photograph was taken, around 1905. The pub closed in 1927. Further down, the Savile Arms is the end building at No. 1 Westgate. Mrs Senior was the landlady at the time.

The Savile Arms, Elland was built in 1748. A carved stone tablet, bearing this date, along with the Savile coat of arms and motto, 'Be Fast', is above the left-hand entrance. Webster's purchased the Savile Arms in 1922 for £5,000.

A horse and cart belonging to the Sowerby Bridge United District Flour Society stands outside the Rawson's Arms, Park Road. Robert Gledhill was the landlord when this photograph was taken in 1904. Two years later, in 1906, Walter Thomas Knowles founded his clay-pipe and chimney-pot manufacturing company on the hillside behind the pub. When the Rawson's Arms closed the building became part of the company's premises.

Taken in 1924, landlord Fred Carter and his wife look on as son Walter holds on to this splendid horse, outside the Golden Fleece at Blackley. The horse, named Boxer, had just won first prize at the Elland Carnival, for 'Best Working Horse'. The inn was one of the John Ainley & Sons, Wappy Spring Brewery houses until Webster's acquired the brewery in 1957.

Looking up Westgate, Elland, the sign for the Fleece Inn can be seen on the building at the top. Most of the property pictured disappeared in clearances of the 1960s including the barn behind the Fleece, the home of 'Leatherty Coit', a carriage said to dash out at midnight pulled by four headless horses and a headless coachman (Leatherty Coit himself), one of many stories connected to this ancient pub.

Originally known as the Great House, the Fleece was built around 1610. This date appears above the back door. The inn once had a bowling green at the front, as seen here. In 1745, General Oglethorpe was sent by General Wade from Wakefield to try to overtake the Jacobean army retreating from Derby. En route and accompanied by some 3,000 troops, they halted at Westgate where George Readyhough, who lived in part of the Great House, provided a tub of galker (a locally brewed ale).

The small building in the centre of this picture, taken in 1869, is the Holywell Green Bar House where tolls were collected in relation to the Salterhebble, Stainland and Sowerby Bridge Trust until 1870. The building behind the Bar House was the Waggon and Horses Inn. With the coming of the railways, and the opening of the nearby Stainland Branch Line in 1875, the inn was renamed the Station Hotel. The pub is now known as the Holywell Inn.

Posing for the camera, these children are standing in Stainland Road, West Vale, near the bottom of Dean Street. On the far side of Dean Street is the Travellers Rest, whilst nearer the camera was the West Vale Tavern, which closed in 1959; Dan Gill and Jemima Collinge were the landlord and landlady at the time.

The horse and cart is standing outside the Shears Inn in West Vale. The building was once the westerly part of Lambert House, a sixteenth-century farmhouse forming part of the Savile estates. The building was turned into an inn sometime between 1825, when Stainland Road was made, and 1836, when a sale of the estate was held in the Shears Inn, the first recorded mention of the inn.

Captioned 'result of drinking cheap beer, Shears Inn', these gents were photographed at the back of the pub in West Vale. On the cart the writing refers to 'Stangers Taxi, West Vale No. 1'.

The Star Inn can be seen on the top left in this picture of Lindwell, Greetland. The photograph, taken in around 1900, shows a horse and cart turning to head up Road End towards the pub: strangely, no driver can be seen with the horse. Perhaps he had gone ahead to get the drinks in?

The Rose and Crown at Greetland is on the left of this picture, which was taken from the hillside opposite the pub. Standing alongside Rochdale Road, the pub has served travellers for many years; its original stone fireplace, with its date of 1725, gives an indication of the age of the property.

The horse and cart waits outside the Rose and Crown having climbed the steep Rochdale Road from West Vale. John Ainley & Sons of the Wappy Springs Brewery bought the Rose and Crown at auction in 1936. In 1957, Webster's purchased the Wappy Springs business and with it acquired nineteen houses, including the Rose and Crown.

This little girl, along with her dog, stands on the steps of the Fleece Inn, Greetland. Charles Clay was the landlord at the time; William Clay was listed as the landlord in 1887 and 1894, suggesting the pub was a family business for quite a number of years.

Not many photographs exist showing the inside of pubs, particularly the taproom. Even more rare is the sight of a taproom like the Fleece Inn, Greetland in this photograph of around 1905. The walls are covered with displays of stuffed birds, with the odd squirrel thrown in.

6

DOWN THE CALDER VALLEY

The Maypole Inn, Warley was originally known as the Horns and dates back over 200 years. The first-known reference to the inn was made in 1773, when Joseph Farrar left the public house known as 'the Horns' to his great-nephews. The children in the picture are sitting on the drinking fountain, one of the many gifts donated to Warley by Mr A.S. McCrea. The fountain was erected in 1900 on the site where the town's maypole once stood. The last maypole – the town's fourth – had been erected in 1888 but was blown over in 1899.

From a glass slide taken by historian H.P. Kendall, this photograph shows three farmers steering their cattle past the side of the Maypole Inn. The picture dates from around 1900, when Fred Jowett was the landlord.

Due to its warren of homes, housing some fifty families, this area of Cote Hill was once known as 'the city'. Situated in the middle of the photograph, facing Burnley Road, is the Rose and Crown Inn, which closed in 1941. Many of the properties in the picture were demolished in the early 1950s.

Landlord Herbert Elliott Smith stands in the doorway of the Brown Cow Inn, Burnley Road. His son Jack is in his arms, whilst his other son, Tony, leans against the wall. The photograph was taken in 1908. In 1935, a major road-widening scheme for Burnley Road was approved by Halifax Council, this included the demolition of the Brown Cow, its license being transferred to the Allan Fold.

Thomas Frost was the landlord of the Peacock Inn, Cote Hill when this photograph was taken, around 1905. The scene is very different these days with the property further along Burnley Road, including the Rose and Crown, demolished. The front of the Peacock is also very different following extensive alterations made to the pub in 1954.

The Friendly Inn, Burnley Road was built by John Turner. The pub has been a welcome stop for travellers for many years. The sign over the building to the right indicates that 'Good Stabling' was being offered when this photograph was taken in around 1906, when Arthur Thomas was the landlord.

Two pubs appear in this photograph of Luddenden Foot. David Pugh was the landlord of the Weavers, the first pub on the right of the picture, listed in a 1905 directory as a beerhouse. James Hurst was the landlord of the licensed premises of the General Rawdon Hotel on the other side of Luddenden Lane. An earlier inn, the Red Lion Hotel, had previously occupied this site. Currently, both the General Rawdon (known more recently as the Coach and Horses) and the Weavers stand vacant and boarded up.

This could be one of the old folks' treats that took place at the Shoulder of Mutton, Midgley for over fifty years. An inn by the name of Broad Stones had previously occupied the site, but was demolished in 1831 by Richard Patchett. He then built a new inn called the Shoulder of Mutton. The Shoulder closed in 1956; the licensee at the time, seventy-five-year-old Alfred Harwood, was told by the then owners, Richard Whitaker's & Sons, that he could remain in the house for the rest of his days. However, when he needed a drink he had to visit the nearby Sportsman Inn, to where the license had been transferred.

The Sportsman Inn faces Towngate at the bottom of Thorney Lane, Midgley. Tom Johnson Horner was the landlord when this postcard was sent from the inn in 1925. The village of Midgley had enjoyed an abundance of pubs and beerhouses but when the Sportsman closed in 1990, following in the footsteps of the Delvers Arms, the Weavers Arms, the Shoulder of Mutton and the Royal George (to name but a few), the village was for the first time without licensed premises.

Pictured here when it was the Luddenden Working Men's Club and Institute, this historic building was built in 1653. During the eighteenth century the building was known as the Wolf Inn. In 1745, during the Jacobite Rebellion, a lone Highlander, one of Bonnie Prince Charlie's army, became detached from the main body of Scots retreating from Derby. Looking for food and drink he came across the Wolf Inn where he was lucky to find a Scottish serving maid called Janet. Knowing of his immediate danger, she convinced him to hide upstairs. The English soldiers arrived shortly afterwards, looking for any Highland stragglers, and searched the inn, but all they found was an open window and a ladder; the Highlander had escaped, along with the maid. Nothing was seen of the pair until three years later: with the country then more settled, Janet and her now husband, Keith Macdonald, returned to tell the story of their escape via Lancashire to Scotland, where they had married. In 1946, the Luddenden Working Men's Club moved to new premises and the building was then used for a number of years as one of Astin Brothers' clothing factories. Unfortunately in 1959, having fallen into disrepair and in a dangerous state, the building was demolished.

The Lord Nelson in Luddenden was built in 1634 as a private residence by Gregory Patchett, replacing an earlier dwelling that had occupied the site. Over the years, the history of the inn has been well documented, perhaps due to its connections with the Brontë family but also because it housed one of the earliest lending libraries in the country. There is some confusion when the library was established: its own library stamp is dated 1781, but a book was found in 1958 that recorded damage to the libraries' books as far back as 1776. The library had many well-known members: William Dearden, 'The Bard of Caldene', local poet, headmaster and one-time president of the Huddersfield Literary and Philosophical Society; the two Leyland Brothers, Francis and Joseph, writer and sculptor respectively; and, amongst others, Patrick Branwell Brontë, the brother of the famous Haworth sisters, who worked at the nearby railway station in Luddenden Foot. Prior to 1805, the pub was known as the White Swan but with the patriotic fever that swept the country following Nelson's victory at Trafalgar, it was renamed in his honour as the Lord Nelson.

This young chap, sitting on his horse, is pictured outside the Royal Oak, Mytholmroyd. The landlord at the time was Lummas Lumb. The building is still standing, on the opposite side of the White Lion, Burnley Road, but no longer operates as a pub.

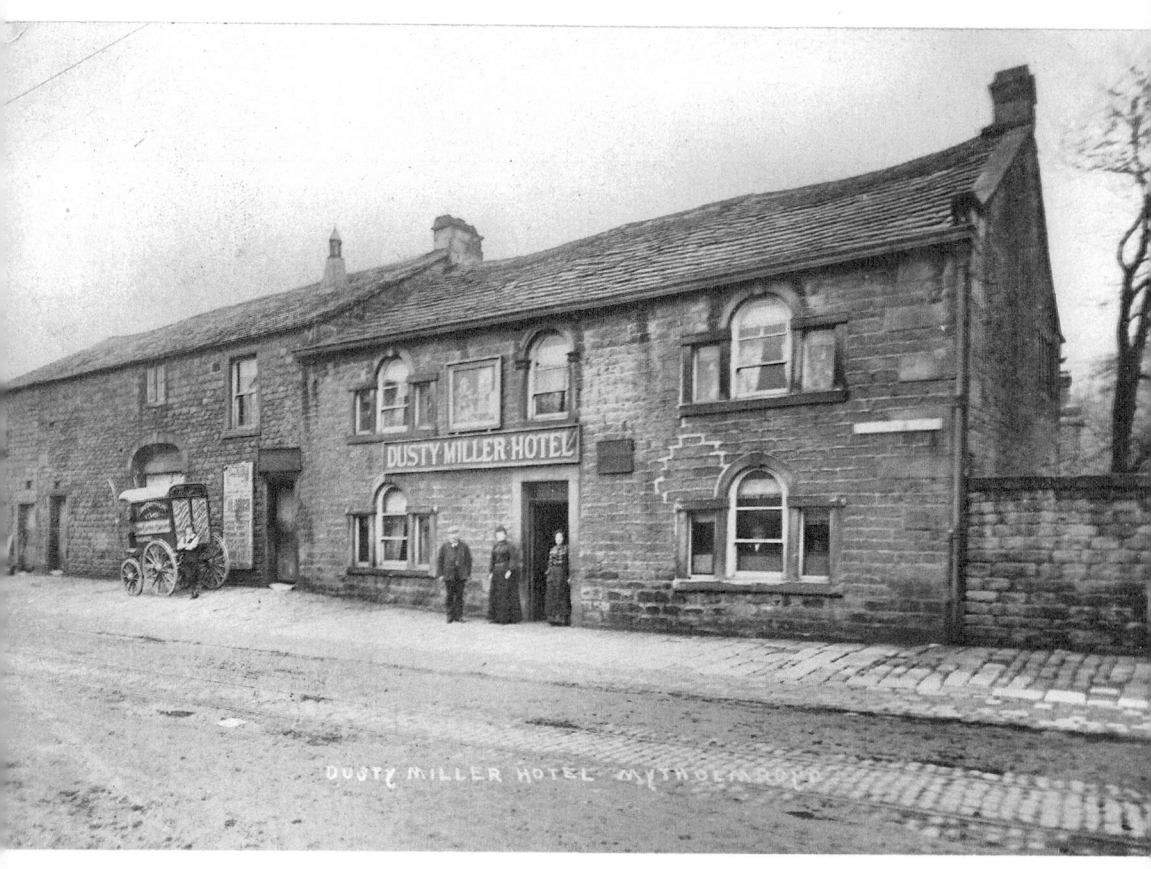

The Dusty Miller, Mytholmroyd was one of the main meeting places of the Cragg Vale Coiners. It was here, following the arrest of their leader, that the coiners plotted to murder excise man William Deighton. Robert Thomas and Matthew Normanton, his murderers, were subsequently hanged in York and their bodies later suspended in chains on Beacon Hill, their right hands pointing to the scene of the murder.

The Sportsman Inn, Gates End, Cragg Vale was bought by Webster's from J. Tetley & Sons for £850 in 1930. The inn, which had originally opened some seventy years earlier as a beerhouse, closed in August 1959.

Once known as the Cragg Vale Inn, the Hinchliffe Arms is named after the family of that name. The family at one point owned several mills in the area including the Victoria, Pepper Bank and Cragg Mills. In the first half of the nineteenth century the Cragg Vale area was notorious for its atrocious working conditions, particularly for its child labour. The Hinchliffe mills were no exception; young children often worked sixteen-hour shifts. It has been recorded that the screams of the children could be heard outside the mills as they were beaten to keep them awake.

The Rochdale Canal opened from Sowerby Bridge to Todmorden in 1798. Around two years later the Foster family of Erringden built the Stubbing Wharf Hotel to serve travellers on the canal and the nearby turnpike road. The area of Stubbing goes back much further to when the trees in the valley were cleared making way for this small hamlet.

The occasion is unknown but these smartly dressed gents, all wearing buttonholes, are posed outside the Stubbing Wharf Hotel. The local cattle market used to be held here twice a month on what is now the car park.

An early view of Bridge Gate, Hebden Bridge, with the sign for the White Swan in the centre of the picture. In the distance the Shoulder of Mutton can be seen. James Crabtree and Walter Medley would have been the respective landlords at the time.

Another inn that helped serve the canal traffic was the Neptune Hotel at Hebble End. Built in the early nineteenth century, the inn has since been converted into two private dwellings. Here we see it in the days when Jonathan Booth was the landlord. Some faces can be seen looking out from the Smoke Room, whilst the little girl stands next to the windows of the Bar Parlour.

The Cross Inn, Towngate was built in the early part of the seventeenth century. Over the years it has been witness to many historic events. The plague of 1631 killed a total of 107 people and, it is said, left the village so deserted that Towngate grew over with grass. During the English Civil War battles took place in Heptonstall and several buildings were burned and razed by the troops of General Mackworth. In 1771 another horrific event is believed to have taken place at the inn: the barbaric killing of Abraham Ingham by the coiners. Another pub, the White Lion can be seen at the top of the street.

This picture, taken in around 1890, shows the Black Bull that was just below the Great North Gate in Heptonstall. Directories show that William Crabtree ran the beerhouse in 1838, Ann Sutcliffe in 1853, Hannah Sutcliffe in 1874 and Hudson Marston in 1905. Following the pub's closure, the building was used as the Heptonstall Working Men's Club until 1972.

7

SOWERBY BRIDGE AND THE RYBURN VALLEY

Ready for a trip, in some luxury, on the Halifax Motor Carriers' 'Pioneer' vehicle. Allan McLean was the landlord of the Golden Lion, Ripponden at the time, licensed to sell 'Ale, Beer, Porter and Neat Wines'. The first known records of the inn date back to 1754, when it was known as Spout Farm and stood alone at the side of the Rochdale to Halifax Road.

These two gents are perhaps pondering whether to go in the Wagon and Horses at No. 74 West Street, Sowerby Bridge. West Street had an abundance of public houses but only the New Inn, now known as the Long Chimney, remains. The Wagon and Horses closed in 1906.

A ladies' day out in a horse-drawn charabanc. The picture was taken over 100 years ago, outside the Royal Oak Inn. The Royal Oak is mentioned in the Sowerby Constable Accounts of 1799; an entry dated 7 July refers to the death of Elizabeth Sutcliffe whose inquest was held at the house of Mr Robert Howarth, 'known by the sign of the Royal Oak, Sowerby Street'.

Tramcar No. 67 has just passed the Woolpack Inn on the left of this photograph. The Woolpack (located on the corner of West Street and Foundry Street) was listed in local trade directories as fully licensed, whereas across the other side of Foundry Street was the West End Tavern, classed as a beerhouse. At the time of this picture Edward Spink ran the Woolpack and Thomas Squire the West End Tavern.

The Waiters Arms is one of the oldest buildings in the district and before the surrounding area was developed would have had open aspects across green fields. C.H. Tordoff in his book *The Warley Story* refers to the premises as Duel (Tuel) Lane as mentioned in a 1598 bond and also in the Greave List of 1624 when Arthur Mawde paid 1s 6d lord's dues for a messuage called Duellane. It was near here, in 1535, that George Crowther was murdered at the instigation of one of the Waterhouse family following a dispute over payment of tithes.

Located on the junction of Sowerby Street and West Street, the Royal Hotel was built to provide accommodation for the railways. The original station and goods yard were opened nearby in 1840; at the time John Marsh was the landlord of the Royal. In this picture two iron posts can be seen in front of the hotel. These were made at the foundry in Foundry Street, using old cannon patterns from the Crimean War.

This area must have represented a challenge for even the most hardened of drinkers. The first pub on the right was the Engineers, followed by the William the Forth. The tram is passing what was the Wharf Hotel on the left. Still on the left, above the Bolton Brow Working Men's Club, was the Oddfellows Arms, the Queen Inn, the White Lion Inn and, still going, the Shepherd's Rest. Whilst on the right, the Prospect Inn can be seen in the centre of the picture with the Brown Cow Inn slightly higher up.

With the rapid growth of Sowerby Bridge, brought about by the opening of the turnpike, the canal and later the railway, a public meeting was held in 1854 at the Bull's Head Hotel to discuss improvements to the town. This resulted in the Sowerby Bridge Local Board of Health being established. The Board was later to use part of the new Town Hall, which opened in 1857. John Naylor of Albion Brewery, Warley owned the Bull's Head in 1863 when he set about rebuilding and modernising the hotel.

The Bull's Head Hotel seen after modernisation and with a new frontage. Arthur Walker was the landlord when this photograph was taken. The sign above the main entrance advertises 'Scratcherd's Perfection Scotch Whiskies'. Scratcherd's operated from Bull Green, Halifax in premises known as the Adega.

Joined by their wives and children, these gents are posed outside the Brown Cow Inn, Bolton Brow. Presumably one of the party is John Edward Hellowell, who was the landlord when the photograph was taken in around 1905.

A more modern view of the Brown Cow Inn, taken in 1965 and this time showing the pub's frontage and adjoining properties. Although the pub closed in 1975, the building is still standing, but all the adjoining properties have been demolished.

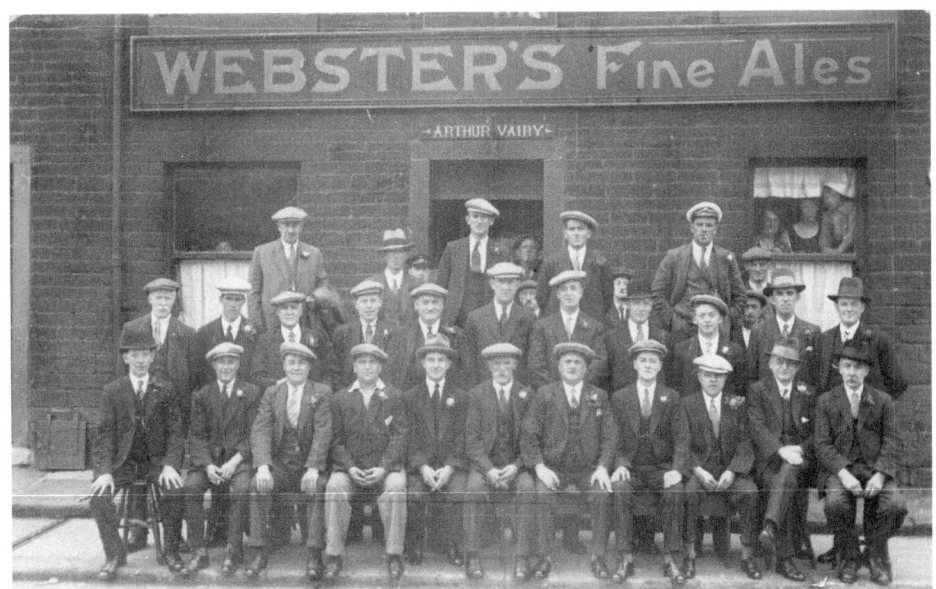

A group of gents pose for a photograph prior to a trip out, whilst their ladies peer out from the windows of the Ram's Head behind them. Arthur Vairy, the landlord in the 1930s, produced an advertising card encouraging customers to 'blot out your dull moments with Webster's Green Label'. More recently this could have referred to the ales of the Ryburn Brewery based at the pub. The Ram was built around 1800, serving the 'new' canal trade; the name 'Ram's Head' is derived from part of a canal barge.

The Navigation Inn, Sowerby Bridge with (presumably) the landlord, William Shoesmith, and his family in the doorway. References to Mearclough Bottom can be found going back as far as 1300, when a mill of that name was located nearby. The first reference to a homestead bearing the same name appears in Manor Court records, held in Halifax, in 1521. Historian H.P. Kendall in his antiquarian paper of 1913 determined that the site was that now occupied by the Navigation Inn.

The West Bottom Tavern was named after its location in Norland. The pub was formed when a number of Quarrymen's Cottages were knocked together. Like many pubs it acquired a nickname, becoming known as the 'Hob', as it was located on Hob Lane. Following restoration in 1975 the pub was renamed the Hobbit.

A picture of the Blue Ball Inn, Norland taken in around 1905, in the days of landlord Colin Robertshaw. The building dates back over 300 years to the early part of the seventeenth century. In 1878, when Joseph Whitaker was the landlord, the inn had a rateable value of £13 15s, with rates payable being £1 2s 11d.

Another Norland pub was the Foresters Arms, which closed in 1939. Here we see a group of regulars with a fine variety of fashions, particularly the different types of hats and headgear. The pub was first licensed at the start of the last century, Joseph Broadbent being the landlord in 1905. An earlier Broadbent, Solomon, was listed as running a beerhouse in Norland in 1894.

Tramcar No. 67 is seen here at the tram terminus outside the Blue Ball Inn, Stile. Ann Naylor was the licensee when this photograph was taken. The Blue Ball closed at the end of 1910. The tram route, which had opened in 1905, ran for another twenty-four years, closing in July 1934.

Perhaps an early meeting of the pipe smokers' club, at least three of the gents sitting on a bench outside the Triangle Inn are enjoying a puff on their pipes. In the background is the hairdresser, wholesale retailer and tobacconist's shop run by George H. Hoyle.

The Triangle Inn dates back to 1767 and is fairly unusual in the fact that it gave its name to the village that sprung up around it. Another photograph in this chapter shows the tram terminus outside the Blue Ball Inn, stopping a few hundred yards short of the Triangle Inn. Tom Mellor, the landlord in the 1930s, was annoyed at this situation, but failed in his attempts to get the route extended. However, when the tram system was dismantled he bought the turning pole from Stile and installed it on the opposite side to the Triangle Inn where it stands today.

The ladies in this picture are reading a sign leaning against the Junction Inn, Ripponden. The inn was built in 1852 by John Garside; it was a temperance hotel, one of the earliest as the temperance movement was still gaining momentum around this period. The steps to the side of the inn once led to the basement where bare-knuckle fighting used to take place.

The Bridge Inn is one of the oldest inns in Yorkshire. Mention is made of 'Robert del Brigg de Soland' in the Wakefield Court rolls of 1313 suggesting even earlier buildings once occupied the site. In 1653, Richard Firth gave the building to Ripponden church, along with other property, on condition that the minister of the chapel was to preach five sermons per year. The inn remained church property until being sold to the brewery in 1897; at the time the church was gaining rent of £24 per annum from the inn.

Another view of the Bridge Inn, Ripponden but taken in the days when it was known as the Old Waterloo Inn. The sign in the window advertises Walkers, Kilmarnock, which helps date the photograph, as the brand was renamed Johnnie Walker in 1908. This is presumably the landlord at the time, J.D. Stott, and his wife.

Originally known as the Stansfeld Arms, the Queen Hotel, Ripponden was erected at the end of the eighteenth century by George Stansfeld. A specific requirement was to ensure it could accommodate large gatherings as the village then had limited facilities; the top floor extended over the whole building. The Ripponden Female Society once held its annual meetings and dinners here: in 1849 they catered for 649 members, spread over several sittings. This photograph dates from the 1860s; a man can be seen posting a letter at the post office next door to the Queen. Miss Bradley, the daughter of the Queen's landlady, was the first official postmistress at Ripponden.

Kinder Fairbairn, on the left, and friends have a drink outside the Commercial Inn, Ripponden. Clearly there was no point wasting precious drinking time, even to stop for the camera. A Ramsden's house, Joe Harry Whiteley was the landlord when this photograph was taken.

Another view of the Commercial Inn – ready to go on a lads' trip out. The Commercial Inn was built in 1860, and known as Glenhaven Cottage. Following refurbishment in the 1980s, the pub, which had long since been known as 'The Besom', adopted the nickname and was renamed the Besom Brush.

The Royal Hotel, Rishworth was built in 1799 and, like the Queen Hotel, built around the same time, the whole of the top storey was made as one large room to provide facilities as a meeting place. The first innkeeper was Thomas Leach, who traded under the sign of the Kings Arms. Isaac Kershaw was landlord in 1844, by which time the inn was known as the Royal Hotel. This name remained until recently when it became the Malthouse.

This motorbike and sidecar are parked outside the Cunning Corner Inn, Rishworth during the days when John Fowler was the landlord. The inn was built in the early nineteenth century and was known as the Boothwood Inn; it was kept in 1806 by Sarah Lucey. In the 1840s it changed its name to the Coach and Horses and in 1857 it was known as the Oddfellows' Arms. In the 1880s it took the name of the Cunning Corner Inn, a name that remained until 2004 when, following restoration, it began trading as the Old Bore.

This group of men are posed outside the Spread Eagle Inn, Rishworth. In 1800 the inn was known as Butts Green. John Henry Priestley, in his Halifax antiquarian paper on Ryburn Valley Inns, 1942, refers to the days when archers practised at the Butts, in the days when everyone was expected to be proficient with the bow and arrow. Sarah Schofield was the landlady at the time this photograph was taken. The inn closed on 31 December 1948.

The first-known reference to the Derby Inn, Rishworth dates from 1822 when John Garside was the landlord. The inn, once the property of Lord Savile, was a popular visiting spot in the days of horse-drawn wagonettes and carriages, with visitors coming from both sides of the Lancashire and Yorkshire border. Alexander George Henley was the landlord when this photograph was taken. The pub now operates as the Turnpike Inn.

Leaning against the doorway of the Fleece Inn, Barkisland, is this perhaps the landlord J. Holroyd Wadsworth pouring himself a drink? Standing alongside an ancient packhorse route, the inn has served needy travellers for over 270 years; the inscription over the door reads I.D.M. 1737.

The original part of the Griffin Inn, Barkisland was built in 1642. Some of the earliest references to the pub can be found in our local directories where John Heward is listed as running the pub in 1822, Christopher Fairbank in 1838, Ann Holroyd in 1853 and John Ward in 1874.

8

THE BREWERIES

A fine display of dray horses at Ramsden's Brewery. At one time the brewery had over thirty horses that were used well into the motor age. In fact it was as late as 1954 when it was announced that the company was to dispense with the final four of its famous horses. The last of the horse keepers was John 'Willy' Steele who was clearly sorry to see Brandy, Duke, Captain and the rest of the stable go, though each went to good homes. For example, Lordy and Rusty who went to working farms in Doncaster and Bingley respectively.

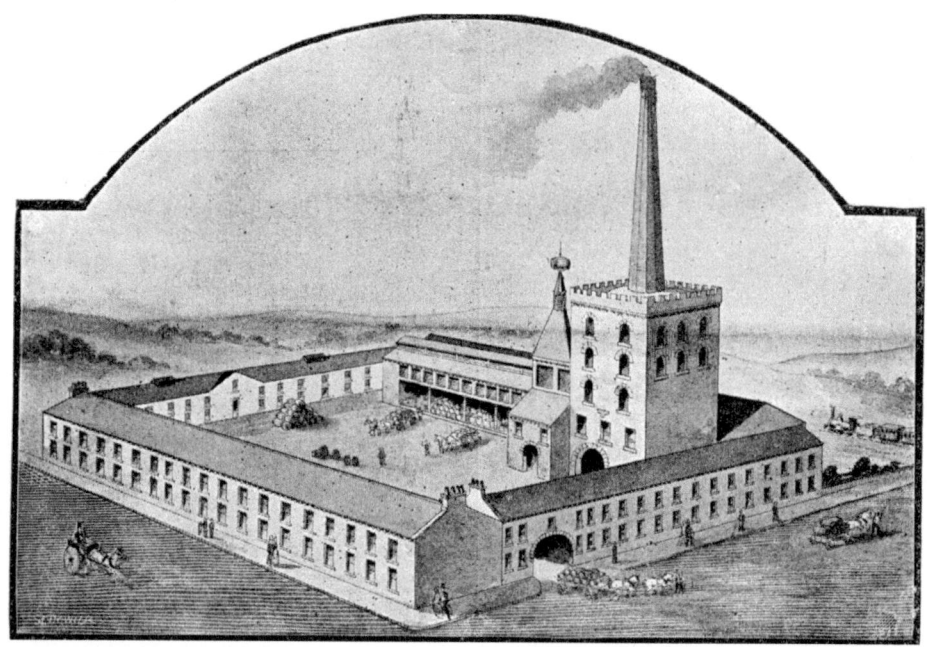

The Red Cross Brewery was built at Rastrick in 1874, with its entrance looking on to Foundry Street. Founded by John Brook and John Booth, the early history of the brewery involved a number of takeovers, the company changing hands several times until 1884 when a Mr Prynn, from Hull, acquired the business. Mr Prynn ran the company until 1889, when he sold it to Samuel Webster & Sons. Prominent in this picture of the brewery is the battlemented tower, and alongside it the barrel shaped weather vane.

Hanging Lee Mill, Ripponden was known as a cotton mill as far back as 1822. The mill was rebuilt following a fire in 1865. In 1897, the property ceased operating as a cotton mill and the machinery was removed. The premises were sold and registered in 1900 as the Sowerby Bridge & District United Club Brewery Co. Ltd. In 1924, it became the Ripponden Free Brewery Co. Ltd.

The large building in the middle of this photograph was the Crown Brewery, which John Eastwood opened in 1876. Standing alongside Bradford Road, Northowram, it was purchased by Henry Bentley of Eshaldwell Brewery, Woodlesford around 1890.

Here we see the Crown Brewery horses well decorated, with the sign on the dray indicating Bentley's Yorkshire Breweries Ltd, Northowram, Halifax. Bentley's became a limited company in 1892, about the same time that this photograph was taken. The brewery closed in 1900, later becoming the Crown Works, occupied by Northowram Tannery Ltd.

Although the Puzzle Hall was classed as a home-brew house rather than a commercial brewery, the sign on this 'dray' clearly shows they supplied families with casks and pint bottles. The gentleman in the picture is likely to have been the owner, Mr John Platt, who was killed in an unfortunate accident on 24 October 1912, falling from the roof of the inn whilst carrying out repairs.

Trade directories show that Levi Walton ran the Puzzle Hall in 1845. By 1887 Schofield Hainsworth had taken over the running of a beerhouse in Hollings Lane, presumably the Puzzle Hall, and was still listed in 1894. Lydia Platt (neé Hainsworth) was landlady by 1905 and was responsible for building the brewery tower that can still be seen today. The brewery was purchased by S.H. Ward & Co. Ltd, of Sheffield, in 1935.

Barrels galore inside the yard of the Stone Trough brewery. T. Boothroyd & Son ran the brewery from 1818 to 1821. In 1837 Peter Beck had taken over and continued to own the brewery until his death about 1861. The brewery then went into the ownership of Lupton, Charnock & Co. until 1881, when Thomas Ramsden purchased the brewery. Prior to this, Thomas Ramsden & Sons had been operating from the Clough Brewery, Mixenden. White's 1881 directory refers to the company in Mixenden as brewers and farmers.

This photograph shows one of those ceremonies which have been lost to our modern ways: 'Cooper Trussing'. Perhaps Raymond Cheetham, pictured here, would have preferred it if it had died out before his own twenty-first birthday and his initiation from apprentice to journeyman cooper. The ceremony took place at Ramsden's Stone Trough Brewery on 6 August 1954.

Another picture taken inside the yard of Ramsden's Stone Trough Brewery (this time showing only one of their many dray horses) which gives an indication of why the Ramsden's horses won so many awards and championships.

Moving into the new motorised era, Ramsden's fleet of wagons line up outside their new garage premises on Powell Street; the brewery is in the background on the other side of Trinity Road. It was many years after this photograph was taken before they completely replaced the traditional horse and dray.

The 'Stonetrough' family walking away with the Challenge Cup. This advertising card would have hung proudly on the back of many of the bars selling Ramsden's ales and stouts in 1932.

Looking down into the yard that was once full of barrels. Ramsden's remained successful at Stone Trough Brewery for over eighty years until Allied Breweries purchased the company in 1964. The last barrel of beer was brewed at Stone Trough in 1967. The brewery buildings and site were subsequently sold to the Halifax Building Society. Here, demolition is well under way in preparation for the building of the Halifax's new head office.

Richard Whitaker commenced his brewing business in 1849 in a cottage, later to become the Stannary Inn. With his growing success as a brewer, he purchased land nearby at Seedlings. He built a new brewhouse and moved production to the new site in 1867. The business continued to grow and further land and property was purchased to enable more buildings and stables to be built. The brewery can be seen here on the left above the Corporation Inn.

Earlier we saw a barrel shaped weather vane on the Red Cross Brewery. In the 1960s Whitaker's went one better with the design of this vehicle, proudly displaying the Cock o' the North, Whitaker's brand name, on the top.

An early advertisement from Whitaker's proclaiming the benefits of its Shire and Standard ales over spirits: 'makes you smile at winter chills'.

In 1968, Whitaker's was purchased by Whitbread & Co. Ltd and ceased brewing the following year. Here we see the Cock o' the North Brewery during demolition in 1973; in the foreground Burdock Way is under construction.

Here we see an advert for Alderson's Ales, 'a healthy, honest beverage'. James Alderson originally operated from the Lower Brear brewery, but due to the company's success moved to new premises at Windmill Hill, Northowram. Production later moved to the Warley premises around 1908, presumably when the brewery took on the Warley Springs name. Thomas Ramsden & Sons bought the brewery in 1919.

A tram approaches the Warley Springs Brewery of James Alderson's. It was originally known as the Victoria Brewery, established by John Naylor in 1858. At some point it changed its name to the Albion Brewery. However, John Naylor was still listed as the owner until the end of the nineteenth century when Halifax Brewery Co. had taken over the business.

Webster's Fountain Head Brewery is prominent in the centre of this photograph looking up the Hebble Valley. Samuel Webster acquired his brewery at Ovenden Wood in 1838, at the age of twenty-five. Perhaps the most famous of the brewery buildings and distinctive in this photograph was the Maltings; this was used on many of the firm's advertising literature. A decision to build their own malt kiln was taken in 1898 and the building was erected over the following two years.

Webster's continued to grow and made a number of purchases of other breweries, many being local such as the Red Cross Brewery, Brighouse (closed 1902); Joseph Stocks, Shibden Head Brewery (1933); Daniel Fielding & Sons, White Castle Brewery, Bradshaw (1961). Here we see the growing floor at the Maltings, Fountain Head.

A wagon belonging to Webster & Sons approaches the bottom of Lister Lane in a parade through the town in the 1960s. Of particular interest is the man on the back of the wagon filling his tankard from the solitary barrel. Why was the barrel marked 'Whitaker's Ales?'

The open countryside around the Ovenden Wood brewery had its own benefits; here we see hundreds of barrels stacked outside ready for use. With the company's continued success, Samuel was joined in 1860 by his three sons Isaac, George Henry and Samuel Green, who became partners, and the firm started trading under the name of Webster & Sons.

9

HALIFAX ARTISTS

A view of Crown Street by Joseph Riddeal Smith as it would have appeared in the middle of the nineteenth century. The coach is outside the old White Swan; Sarah Daxon being the licensee at the time. A timetable, dated 1830, showed regular departures and arrivals throughout the day, starting with the *Hope* to London, via Huddersfield and Sheffield at 5 a.m. This was followed an hour later by the *Perseverance* to Manchester via Todmorden. Other destinations are listed with the final arrival being at 9 p.m., the 'shuttle' from Blackpool.

John Horner included this picture of the Malt Shovel, Northgate in his 1835 portfolio *Views of Buildings in the Town and Parish of Halifax*. The inn was built in 1629, and the scene shows its frontage, on Northgate, looking towards the town centre. The farmer and his sheep would be passing Woolshops and Old Market. The buildings were demolished in 1824, with the Malt Shovel being rebuilt but much further back. In 1852, an advertisement for the inn stated that Benjamin Milne, formerly of the Wellington Inn, Elland had caused 'alterations and improvements intended for the comfort and accommodation of travellers and others as cannot fail to give satisfaction. A picture gallery is now open, and a stock of wines, spirits and stouts are purchased direct and selected with peculiar judgement and cash. N.B. Stabling for forty horses.' The carved stone to the top right of the inn was salvaged and subsequently, when the second Malt Shovel was closed, in 1913 the stone was built into a wall at the back of the Brewers Cellar in Wade Street.

John Horner was born on 23 March 1784, at the time his parents were living in a cottage in Stone Trough Lane, now Trinity Road. This view by Horner is taken from the window of the famous 'Edwards of Halifax' bookshop and looks up Old Market, as it would have appeared in 1800. On the right, a horse can be seen in the entrance to the Union Cross Yard. Opposite the Union Cross is the Spread Eagle and further up on the same side was the Turks Head. It was here in 1643 that Thomas Stockdale wrote the official despatch to the House of Commons describing the battle of Adwalton Moor, where General Thomas Fairfax was defeated and retreated to Halifax.

This drawing of the Waggoner's Inn, Northgate by J.R. Smith is taken from an original sketch made by his father, Mr Isaac Smith. Isaac was the innkeeper when Joseph was born here in 1837. Joseph described this area as the 'nucleus of the carrying trade in Halifax prior to the introduction of the railways'. The inn occupied the second and third gables and was entered via steps in the passage. Smith gives a clue to the exact location of the Waggoner's, by including the Wade Street sign on the right, placing the inn between the present Crossley Street and Broad Street.

Another drawing of the Waggoner's Inn, during a period when it was customary to keep goats in the stables attached to larger inns. Mr Smith's goat can be seen having a 'dispute' with a dog, whilst the lads struggle to pull the goat back. The goat grew to a very large size, terrorising regulars and passers-by to such an extent it was sold to George Wombwell's Travelling Menagerie to be exhibited as an outsize goat.

This print by Smith shows Silver Street, from Hall End, in 1868. On the left of the picture, the line of the pavement is spoilt by the White Lion, which was demolished in 1882. Opposite, a horse-drawn omnibus can be seen outside the Globe Inn. The inn was the starting point for carriers along the Calder Valley, including Hebden Bridge, Todmorden and Burnley. Fox Ginnel, on the left, is on the line of the present Commercial Street, which was not completed until 1891.

Another view of Silver Street by Smith – or should that be 'drinker's paradise'? Narrowing the road in the distance is the White Lion, round the corner on the left was the Globe Inn and on the right the Black Swan. Further up the street were the Golden Plough and the Black Lion inns. Still in the picture, a delivery is being made to the Woodman Inn, on the left – and if that was not enough, a directory of the period lists three wine and spirit merchants, including James and Richard Thomas (seen here opposite the Woodman).

This view of the Banqueting Hall at the Old Cock Hotel appeared in John Leyland's *Ancient Buildings in the Parish of Halifax*. His description stated that the house was one of the largest ever built in the town. Erected in the time of Elizabeth I, its principal façade was to the east and commanded an uninterrupted view of the hillside at the foot of the town. Pastures and clumps of trees extended from the house to the brook, then unpolluted, and stored with trout; to the south were gardens and orchards. How things change.

This picture by Leyland shows the White Swan, and adjacent houses, in Crown Street, as they would have appeared in 1750. The narrative, in Leyland's portfolio of Halifax buildings of 1879, states that the picture 'very accurately represents the general character of our street architecture in ancient times'. The picture was 'restored from evidence discovered on their demolition in 1859-60'.

Another view by Leyland, this time of the Spread Eagle Inn, Old Market and as Leyland himself put it – now destroyed. This was another inn linked to the Yorkshire Coiners and referred to in the evidence of innkeeper Bates, 'there is also a set of people that come from Howarth to the Spread Eagle in Halifax, which if any will be honest and inform; could lead you into Howarth, Bradford, Leeds and Wakefield', an indication of how widespread coining had become.

Henry Raphael Oddy was another respected local artist whose sketches included many of our hostelries. Here we see Cow Green, an area renowned for its public houses, drawn by Oddy in the 1890s. On the left was the Craven Heifer, which closed in 1920; next door was the King's Head, closed in 1968, and a couple of doors away was the Lord Nelson, closed in 1919. Also in the vicinity were the Brown Cow and Black Bull. The reason that so many inns were located within such close proximity of each other was that Cow Green functioned as a cattle market until 1858. Obviously taking your livestock to market was a thirsty business.

Here we see the Black Swan on Silver Street. Around 1830, the Ferry Bridge Court Club held their meetings here. One of their unique customs was that should a member break a rule he was turned upside down and any coins that dropped from his pocket were spent on drink.

The Nags Head, another drawing by Oddy, in a state of disrepair shortly prior to its demolition in 1884. The beerhouse stood at the bottom of King Cross Street, at the bottom of Hopwood Lane. In 1867, during repairs to the inn, an orange-coloured banner dated 1688 was found in a hole in one of the old chimneys; its inscriptions were 'deliver from Church and State' and 'To the glorious memory of 1688 and 1690'. The banner was never claimed, so why such a historical relic was hidden in the Nags Head is unlikely ever to be known.

Born in London in 1864, Arthur Comfort spent his latter years in Halifax, as art master at Heath Grammar School, and of Sowerby Bridge and Hebden Bridge secondary schools. This picture of the Shears Inn, Paris Gates appeared in his work, *Sketches of Old Halifax*, published in 1912. Comfort states in the book, 'this ancient inn formerly stood at the bottom of sloping green fields; now its situation is under the towering Shaw Lodge Mills'.

This picture by Comfort is of the Waterhouse Arms Yard; the pub itself was round the corner on the right, on Nelson Street. H. Ling Roth refers to the days of public flogging in Halifax, in his *Yorkshire Coiners* book, published in 1906 – 'every Saturday at high noon, when the floggings took place, a man would be tied to a cart and flogged from the Waterhouse Arms to the Upper George Inn, on arrival at the inn the man's lacerated back was rubbed with salt.'

Cuthbert Crossley, born in Halifax in 1883, sketched many Halifax pubs. Here we see his view of the Union Cross Yard. In Oliver Heywood's diaries, 1679, he refers to James Mitchell of Crow Nest, Lightcliffe who 'went backwards in the world, mortgaged his house, removed to Halifax, kept an inn at the Cross but got surfeit with drinking, which cost him his life.' A later entry refers to his widow having built a cocking-house at a cost of £32 at the back of the inn. In 1680, a five-day cockfight was held, interrupted at times by much fighting in the crowd. This was only quelled when the landlady's son drew his rapier and threatened to run through the next man to make a blow.

Cuthbert Crossley's atmospheric view of the Oak Room in the Old Cock was drawn in 1933. Built in the sixteenth century as a town house, there has been much debate over the years as to who actually built it. The many clues clearly indicate it was one of the Savile family; but different historians have gone between Sir Henry Savile of Stainland and William Savile of Copley. Historian T.W. Hanson produced a convincing argument that it was the latter.

The Lower George as drawn by Cuthbert Crossley around 1932. It was in a house located in the Lower George Yard that John Crossley first lived when he married Martha Turner; at the time he was working at the carpet works of Job Lee. John would go on to found the largest carpet mills in the world.

This picture of the old Talbot Hotel is unique in this section of Crossley's pictures as all the others are taken from his original prints. This is actually taken from Crossley's tracing paper, presumably so he could reproduce the picture; it is reproduced here using more modern technology. Perhaps the most famous of meetings that took place at the Talbot was on 28 November 1769 when Lord Rockingham, on behalf of the Government, met the justices and gentlemen of the district to discuss the best way to stop the coiners and to assist in finding the murderers of William Deighton.

Other titles published by The History Press

Around Halifax
STEPHEN GEE

This fascinating volume by the author of this present collection contains more than 180 postcards, photographs and rare archive images of Halifax in days gone by, many of which have never before appeared in print. Each image is accompanied by a detailed caption, and every aspect of life in the area is covered, from school life and social events to local industries and institutions. It will delight visitors and residents alike.

978 07524 0396 0

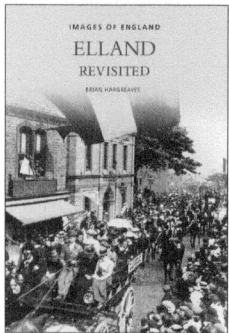

Elland Revisited
BRIAN HARGREAVES

This collection of archive images offers an intriguing and nostalgic insight into life in the town of Elland over the last 100 years. From local events and familiar institutions to the days of the Second World War and the years that followed, it celebrates and remembers the area in days gone by. Filled with rare postcard and photographic views, it will delight all who know the town.

978 07524 4145 0

Olde Yorkshire Punishments
HOWARD PEACH

This richly illustrated work provides a fascinating glimpse into the dark world of Yorkshire punishments through the centuries. All forms of punishment are covered, ranging from the gruesome and extreme to the downright peculiar: capital and corporal, state-sanctioned and some, like the little girl forced to wear a sign labelled 'thief' for scrumping apples from the local rectory, that were most definitely not. This fascinating volume will appeal to all those wishing to discover more about the county's intriguing past.

978 07524 4661 5

Sunny Vale Pleasure Gardens A Postcard From Sunny Bunces
CHRIS HELME

Sunny Vale Pleasure Gardens, near Brighouse, was the Belle Vue or Alton Towers of West Yorkshire. With boating lakes, train and fairground rides, fireworks, a helter-skelter and, of course, beautiful gardens, it was a hugely popular attraction for more than 75 years. This collection of more than 180 images, complemented by reminiscences of the Gardens throughout their long history, will delight all who remember visiting as a child and provide a fascinating insight into this vanished, but not-forgotten, institution.

978 07524 4355 3

If you are interested in purchasing other books published by The History Press, or in case you have difficulty finding any History Press books in your local bookshop, you can also place orders directly through our website:

www.thehistorypress.co.uk